COLONIAL AMERICA HISTORY FOR KIDS

WHAT WAS IT LIKE TO TRAVEL IN THE MAYFLOWER?

Children's History Books

BABY PROFESSOR

EDUCATION KIDS

Speedy Publishing LLC
40 E. Main St. #1156
Newark, DE 19711
www.speedypublishing.com
Copyright 2017

In this book, we're going to cover what it was like to travel on the ship called the Mayflower. So, let's get right to it!

The journey of the pilgrims to America began in the year 1608. At that time, the official church in England was the Anglican Church. King James I had sanctioned this religion and the Puritan beliefs of the pilgrims were considered treason against England.

James I of England

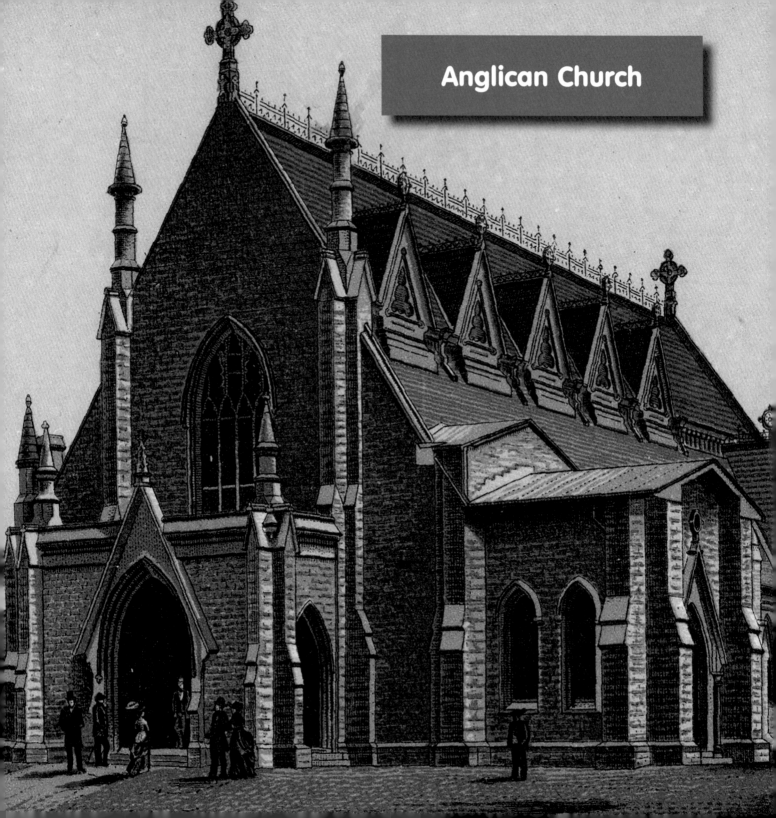

Anglican Church

The pilgrims didn't want to be imprisoned. They wanted to live somewhere where they could practice their religion without fear of consequences. They were called Separatists because they wanted to separate themselves from the official church in England.

First they traveled to Holland, but they weren't happy with their situation there. So they came back to England in 1620 and made the difficult decision to seek a new home in America.

WHY DID THE PILGRIMS COME TO AMERICA?

Our country was founded by individuals who wanted religious freedom. This simply means that they wanted to be able to practice their religion without any interference from the government or other citizens. They wanted a community that supported their beliefs. They knew that the trip to America would be very difficult.

At the time, the only way to get to America was by ship. Their trip would be over 3,000 miles long and they knew there was a considerable risk that they might perish along the way.

Replica of Mayflower II

WHERE DID THEY BOARD THE MAYFLOWER?

The pilgrims had made their decision. They would board a ship bound for America! Unfortunately, these adventurous passengers began to have problems at the very beginning of their trip. They left Southhampton, England on August 5, 1620. Their group was on two different ships.

The first ship was the Mayflower and the second ship was the Speedwell. They were quickly forced back to port in the city of Dartmouth when the Speedwell starting taking on water. They tried a second time as well, but the Speedwell began to leak again and they returned to port again, this time in Plymouth, England.

Mayflower Ship model

WHAT ROUTE DID THEY TAKE ON THEIR JOURNEY?

Once they landed in Plymouth they decided that they didn't want to wait for the Speedwell to be repaired. They crowded all 102 passengers on the Mayflower and departed the port on September 6, 1620. Some of these passengers were pilgrims and some were not.

Cape Cod

Their plan was to land in Virginia. As they were sailing across the Atlantic Ocean, fierce storms knocked them off their mapped-out course. After 66 days onboard the Mayflower, they saw the land that is now called Cape Cod off the bow of the ship. This location was 600 miles north of where they had intended to be and it was now nearly winter. They disembarked on November 9, 1620 and decided to stay.

DID ANYONE PERISH ON THE JOURNEY?

Only one person died on the journey and a little boy was born. His parents named him Oceanus to commemorate the journey.

Plymouth Harbor

WHAT IS PLYMOUTH ROCK?

Plymouth Rock is an important symbol of the freedom and democracy in America. In 1741, over one hundred years after the Mayflower arrived in America, a boulder in Plymouth Harbor was marked as the spot where the pilgrims first came on land.

N o one knows for sure whether it's really the spot where the pilgrims landed, but it's still become an American symbol for the quest for those who want a better life and are willing to make sacrifices to achieve it.

Plymouth Rock

William Bradford

WHAT WAS THE MAYFLOWER COMPACT?

William Bradford, the leader of the pilgrim group got the male settlers in the pilgrim as well as those in the non-pilgrim group to discuss their governing rules before they got off the Mayflower.

He wanted to make sure that the pilgrims would be able to practice their religion as they had planned. They agreed on a document that they called the "Mayflower Compact." All the male settlers had to sign the document before they traveled to shore.

Mayflower Compact

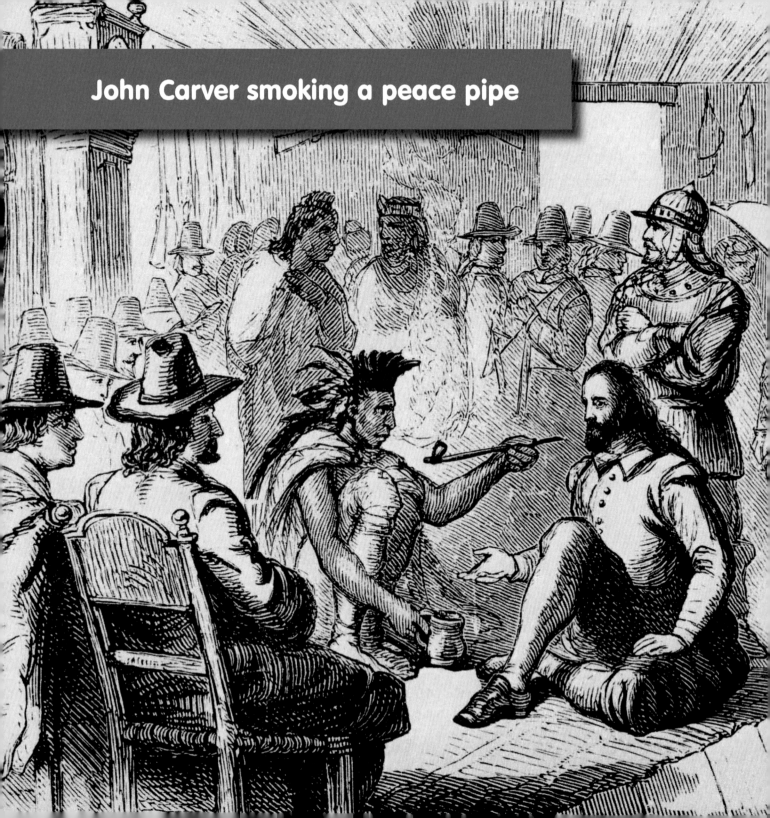

John Carver smoking a peace pipe

Women were not allowed to sign legal documents or vote at that time. They voted John Carver as the first governor of their new colony. This document represented the first sample of a written constitution in America and was the foundation for democratic rule in the American colonies.

HOW BIG WAS THE MAYFLOWER?

It's believed that the Mayflower had been sailing on the seas for about a dozen years before the pilgrims used it for traveling to America. The ship weighed about 180 tons. It was 25 feet wide and its length was 106 feet.

It had a good-sized deck of about 80 feet long. The ship had three different types of masts. There was a front mast, a middle mast, and a back mast. The front mast was called a foremast. The middle mast was called the main-mast. The back mast was called the mizzen.

WHERE DID THE PILGRIMS AND OTHER PASSENGERS SLEEP?

The Mayflower was a cargo ship and was not really designed to take a lot of passengers. The ship was divided into five major areas:

Between decks—This is the area where the passengers stayed for most of the journey. It was also the area where they slept for the night. This part of the ship was called the gun deck as well.

Cabin– This was the area where the captain and his crew had their sleeping quarters.

Steerage– This was the area where the steering mechanism was located. The captain was responsible for steering the ship.

Cargo hold–This area was at the bottom portion of the ship. This was where supplies and other cargo were stored.

Forecastle– This was the food preparation and storage area.

WHAT WAS IT LIKE ON THE MAYFLOWER?

Being a passenger on the Mayflower was not for the faint of heart. During the second half of their journey, the seas got very rough. Since there was always a risk of being thrown overboard, when the weather was rough, the passengers stayed below deck.

The quarters were damp, dark, and probably very smelly since a bucket was the only way you could relieve yourself. The ceiling was only about 5 feet tall.

F amilies tried to set up some makeshift dividers but it was a very uncomfortable situation. When the weather was stormy, they were stuck in the between decks area for days on end with no fresh air while the ship was buffeted about by rocking waves. Seasickness was rampant and it's no wonder that when they spotted land they decided to stay there instead of traveling on.

To make the crowding and smells even worse, there were animals and livestock on the ship as well because they would be needed to provide food for the settlers once they reached land.

During the first part of the journey, the pilgrims tried to convert other passengers to their religious beliefs. This didn't go well and there was a lot of tension. The non-pilgrim passengers were coming to America for freedom as well so they didn't want to be preached to or converted.

Mayflower Compact

Eventually, everyone realized that they should put their governing rules in a document and that's when they started to work on the Mayflower Compact. It was the beginning of the separation of church and state.

WHAT DID THEY EAT WHILE ON BOARD?

When it wasn't raining, the passengers had hot food that was prepared on the deck of the ship. When they couldn't eat on deck, down below they had beef that was salted, fish that was salted as well, hard tack, which was a type of dried biscuit, and other dried, salted vegetables like beans and peas. They also had beer, which they believed was safer than water to drink.

WHAT DID THE PASSENGERS DO?

The passengers were responsible for preparing their own foods and tending to those who were seasick. Almost everyone on the voyage was quite seasick at one point or another. Mothers mended clothes and children played games. The Separatists met together and prayed.

HOW BIG OF A CREW DID THE MAYFLOWER HAVE?

The Mayflower had about 25-30 members on the captain's crew. They were always occupied trying to keep the ship in good running order. The captain, his name was Christopher Jones, was responsible for steering and navigating the ship and he had a number of experienced seamen, called Masters Mates, to support his work.

Christopher Jones Statue

There was an onboard surgeon and a cook to prepare food for the crew. There were four quartermasters who took care of the ship's cargo and a specialized

crew member called a boatswain who was responsible for the rigging and sails of the ship.

WHERE DID THE PILGRIMS SETTLE?

Once they arrived, the pilgrims began to explore the coast of the land we now know as New England to find a suitable place to live. They found a good location with a harbor that had calm waters.

There was a nearby river they could use for fresh water and flat lands that were suitable for farming. They began to build a village there and called their new home Plymouth colony after the port in England they had left before they came to America.

Awesome! Now you know more about what it was like to travel on the Mayflower. You can find more American History books from Baby Professor by searching the website of your favorite book retailer.

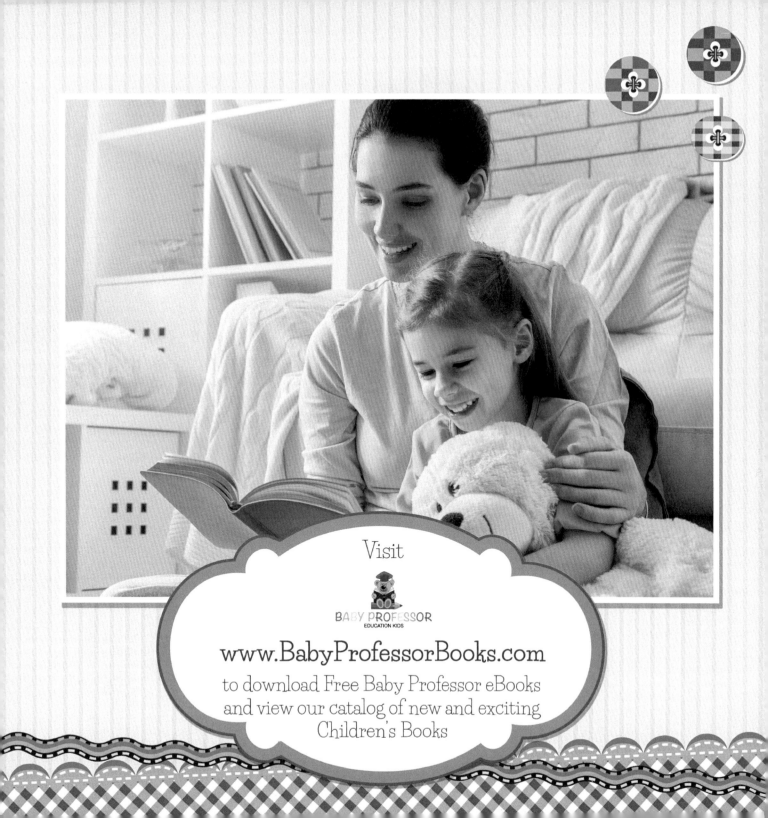

Visit

BABY PROFESSOR
EDUCATION KIDS

www.BabyProfessorBooks.com

to download Free Baby Professor eBooks
and view our catalog of new and exciting
Children's Books

Made in the USA
Middletown, DE
08 February 2018